MILITARY AIRCRAFT

F/A-18
SUPER
HORNET

BY JOHN HAMILTON

VISIT US AT
WWW.ABDOPUBLISHING.COM

Published by ABDO Publishing Company, PO Box 398166, Minneapolis, MN 55439.
Copyright ©2012 by Abdo Consulting Group, Inc. International copyrights reserved in all countries. No part of this book may be reproduced in any form without written permission from the publisher. A&D Xtreme™ is a trademark and logo of ABDO Publishing Company.

Printed in the United States of America, North Mankato, Minnesota.
102011
012012

Editor: Sue Hamilton
Graphic Design: Sue Hamilton
Cover Design: John Hamilton
Cover Photo: U.S. Navy
Interior Photos: Department of Defense-pgs 4-5, 12 (inset); Defense Video & Imagery Distribution System-pgs 2-3, 6-7, 8-9, 22-23, & 24-25; United States Air Force-pgs 1 & 28-29; United States Navy-pgs 10-19, 19 (inset), 20, 21, 26-27, 30-31, & 31;

ABDO Booklinks
Web sites about Military Aircraft are featured on our Book Links pages. These links are routinely monitored and updated to provide the most current information available. Web site: www.abdopublishing.com

Library of Congress Cataloging-in-Publication Data

Hamilton, John, 1959-
   F/A-18 Super Hornet / John Hamilton.
      p. cm. -- (Xtreme military aircraft)
   Includes index.
   ISBN 978-1-61783-270-3
   1. Hornet (Jet fighter plane)--Juvenile literature. I. Title.
   UG1242.F5H3557 2012
   623.74'63--dc23

                           2011042340

TABLE OF CONTENTS

F/A-18 SUPER HORNET

The United States Navy's **F/A-18 Super Hornet** is a combat-proven strike fighter. Launched from aircraft carriers, it can attack targets on land or sea. It can also defend the U.S. fleet from enemy aircraft, day or night, even in bad weather.

XTREME FACT

F/A-18 Super Hornets are nicknamed "Super Bugs" by United States Navy pilots and personnel.

Two Super Hornets fly over the aircraft carrier USS Ronald Reagan.

MISSION: AIR-TO-AIR

In its role as a fighter aircraft, the F/A-18 Super Hornet is used mainly to escort other planes and to protect the Navy's fleet from enemy aircraft.

MISSION: AIR-TO-GROUND

When the F/A-18 Super Hornet is used in its attack role, it engages enemy ground targets, both on land or at sea. It may attack enemy bases, or be used as "close air support," helping friendly ground forces against troops or armored vehicles.

A U.S. Navy F/A-18 Super Hornet flies over Afghanistan. It is used as an attack aircraft, as well as a fighter.

XTREME FACT

Super Hornets can carry up to 17,750 pounds (8,051 kg) of weapons.

9

F/A-18 SUPER HORNET FAST FACTS

F/A-18E/F Super Hornet Specifications

Function:	Multi-role attack and fighter aircraft
Service Branch:	U.S. Navy
Manufacturer:	Boeing
Length:	60.3 feet (18.4 m)
Height:	16 feet (4.9 m)
Wingspan:	44.9 feet (13.7 m)
Maximum Takeoff Weight:	66,000 pounds (29,937 kg)
Airspeed:	Mach 1.8-plus
Ceiling:	50,000-plus feet (15,240 m)
Combat Range:	1,275 nautical miles (1,467 miles, or 2,361 km)

ORIGINS

The F/A-18E/F Super Hornet is an improved version of the original F/A-18 Hornet (models A through D). The original Hornet first flew with the United States Navy in 1983.

An early test flight of the U.S. Navy's Hornet.

The Super Hornet is a modern upgrade. It carries more weapons, and has an increased flight range because of its bigger internal fuel tank. It also has larger wings and more powerful twin engines. The Super Hornet entered service with the Navy in 1999. Many original Hornets are still flying, but will eventually be phased out.

F/A-18C Hornet

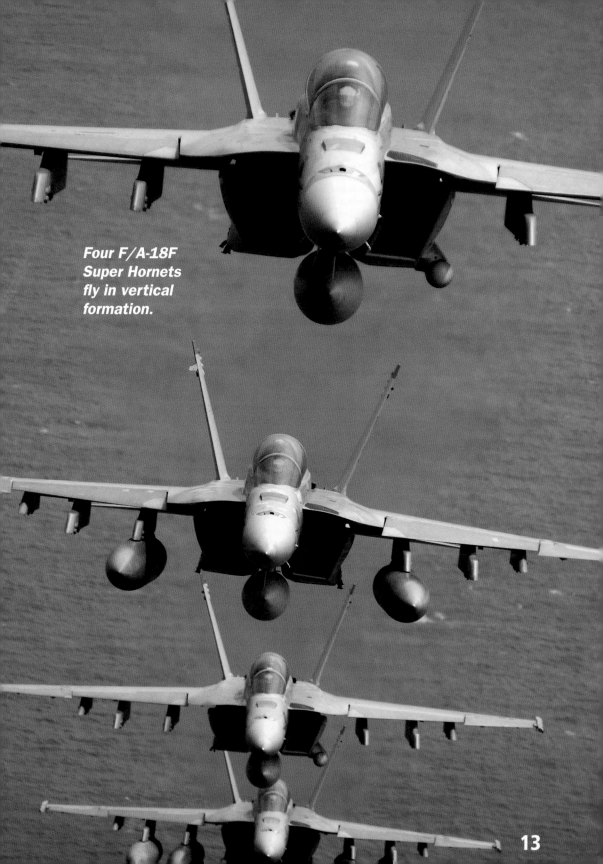

Four F/A-18F Super Hornets fly in vertical formation.

VERSIONS

The two most common versions of the Super Hornet include models E and F. The F/A-18E Super Hornet is a single-seat version. The F/A-18F has two seats, one for a pilot and the other for a weapon systems officer.

CAPT JAMES BYNUM
CAG

WARNING
THIS AIRCRAFT CONTAINS A CARTRIDGE
ACTUATED EMERGENCY ESCAPE SYSTEM
EQUIPPED WITH EXPLOSIVE CHARGES
SEE APPLICABLE MAINTENANCE MANUAL
FOR COMPLETE INSTRUCTIONS

A pilot gives the thumbs up for takeoff in an F/A-18E Super Hornet.

The Super Hornet is sometimes called "Rhino" because of its large nose.

An F/A-18F Super Hornet takes off from the deck of an aircraft carrier.

GROWLER

The EA-18G Growler is an electronic warfare version of the Super Hornet. Growlers carry special equipment that "jams" enemy electronics, making friendly planes harder to shoot down. Growlers can jam enemy radar from a long distance.

An air crew trains in an EA-18G Growler aircraft. In addition to jamming enemy radar, Growlers can also escort friendly planes and carry out attack missions.

TANKER ROLE

One advantage of the Super Hornet over its predecessor is its bigger fuel tank, which greatly extends its range. In addition, Super Hornets can be fitted with an aerial refueling system that allows it to refuel other aircraft. They can also carry large external fuel tanks under their wings. Super Hornets that act as refueling escorts are armed with missiles so they can protect themselves if attacked.

A Super Hornet refuels an EA-6B Prowler.

Refueling tanks, known as "drop tanks," are mounted on an F/A-18F Super Hornet.

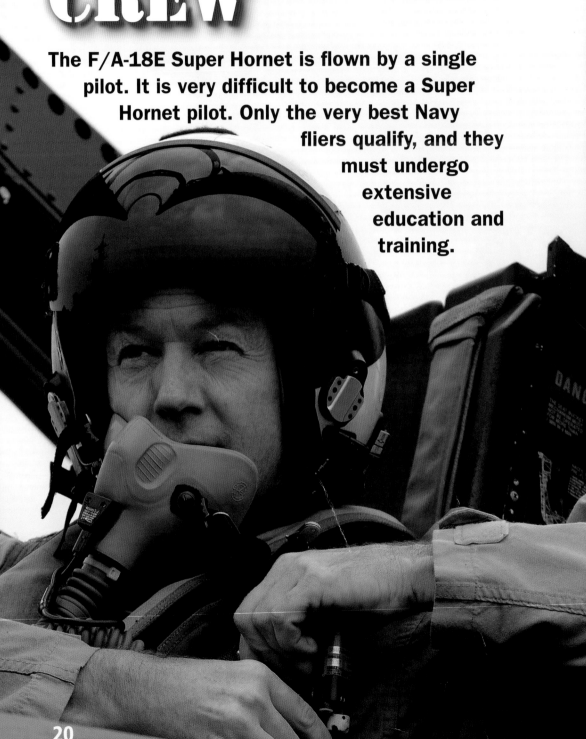

CREW

The F/A-18E Super Hornet is flown by a single pilot. It is very difficult to become a Super Hornet pilot. Only the very best Navy fliers qualify, and they must undergo extensive education and training.

The F/A-18F Super Hornet has a crew of two. The aircraft is usually configured with the pilot sitting in front. In back sits a weapon systems officer.

LTJG C.B. GUNNISON

LT P.E. LINK

AEAN KELLARK
WASHINGTON, D.C.

XTREME FACT

The weapon systems officer tracks enemy targets on sophisticated computer and radar screens, freeing the pilot to put his or her full attention to flying the aircraft.

ENGINE

F/A-18 Super Hornets use two General Electric F414-GE-400 turbofan engines, which produce 44,000 pounds of thrust (195,722 Newtons), much more than previous-generation Hornets. This is one reason Super Hornets can carry more weapons. It also allows them to return to their aircraft carriers and land safely even when carrying heavy loads of unused bombs and missiles.

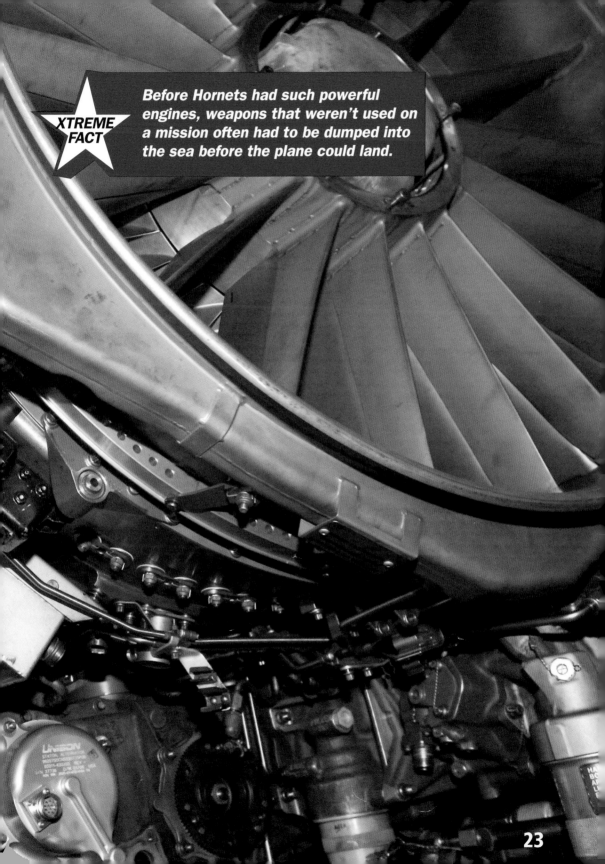

Before Hornets had such powerful engines, weapons that weren't used on a mission often had to be dumped into the sea before the plane could land.

STEALTH

When the F/A-18E/F Super Hornet was redesigned, engineers took advantage of new stealth technology that wasn't available when the original Hornet was first built. Super Hornets are fitted with special baffles placed in front of the engines that reduce radar reflections. Changes to the airframe also reduced the Super Hornet's profile on enemy radar.

Although not designed to be true "stealth" fighters, Super Hornets are hard for the enemy to detect on radar and shoot down.

An F/A-18E Super Hornet prepares to land on an aircraft carrier.

WEAPONS

Super Hornets are very versatile fighters. Many types of "smart" bombs and missiles (precision-guided weapons) can be attached to 11 weapons stations.

A sailor inspects an AIM-9X Sidewinder missile before the launch of a Super Hornet.

Weapon types include AIM-9 Sidewinder and AIM-7 Sparrow missiles for air-to-air combat, Harpoon anti-ship missiles, JSOW glide bombs, Maverick air-to-ground missiles, plus several other standard bombs and rockets.

XTREME FACT

Super Hornets are also armed with a 20mm Vulcan cannon mounted in the aircrafts' nose. The Vulcan fires 6,600 rounds per minute. It can be used against enemy aircraft, or strafe enemy targets on the ground.

COMBAT HISTORY

F/A-18 Super Hornets have flown combat missions during the wars in Iraq and Afghanistan. Super Hornets dropped precision-guided bombs on Iraqi and Taliban targets. They also flew aerial refueling missions. Super Hornets have also flown missions off the coast of Somalia.

A United States Navy F/A-18F Super Hornet flies over Afghanistan in support of Operation Enduring Freedom in 2011.

GLOSSARY

AIRCRAFT CARRIER

A large warship that is a base for aircraft, which take off and land on its deck. F/A-18 Super Hornets serve on United States Navy aircraft carriers such as the USS *Abraham Lincoln* and the USS *Dwight D. Eisenhower.*

AIRFRAME

The body of an aircraft, minus its engine.

MACH

A common way to measure the speed of an aircraft when it approaches or exceeds the speed of sound in air. An aircraft traveling at Mach 1 is moving at the speed of sound, about 768 miles per hour (1,236 kph) when the air temperature is 68 degrees Fahrenheit (20 degrees C). An aircraft traveling at Mach 2 would be moving at twice the speed of sound.

NAUTICAL MILE

A standard way to measure distance, especially when traveling in an aircraft or ship. It is based on the circumference of the Earth, the distance around the equator. This large circle is divided into 360 degrees. Each degree is further divided into 60 units called "minutes." A single minute of arc around the Earth is one nautical mile.

POUNDS OF THRUST

A way to measure the amount of force generated by aircraft engines (and other types of engines). The unit of measurement is usually in pounds (the metric equivalent is a unit called the Newton, named after the scientist Sir Isaac Newton). A pound of thrust is the amount of force needed to accelerate one pound of material 32 feet (9.8 m) per second every second (feet per second per second). One pound of thrust (32 feet per second per second) is the same as the acceleration of Earth's gravity.

PRECISION-GUIDED WEAPON

Precision-guided weapons, also called "smart bombs," are bombs or missiles that can be steered in midair toward their targets. The F/A-18 Super Hornet can fire several kinds of precision-guided weapons, or "munitions." These include bombs and missiles that are guided by lasers, radar, or satellite signals.

RADAR

A way to detect objects, such as aircraft or ships, using electromagnetic (radio) waves. Radar waves are sent out by large dishes, or antennas, and then strike an object. The radar dish then detects the reflected wave, which can tell operators how big an object is, how fast it is moving, its altitude, and its direction. F/A-18 Super Hornets use modern stealth construction to minimize their radar reflection, making them very difficult for enemy forces to detect.

STRAFE

When low-flying aircraft attack objects on the ground, usually with rapid-firing machine guns. F/A-18 Super Hornets use a 20mm Vulcan Gatling gun mounted in their nose to strafe ground targets.

INDEX